Skateboa

Contents	Page
Skateboard fun	2-3
Ollie	4-5
Kick flip	6-7
Rail slide	8-9
Handstand	10-11
On the half pipe	12-13
Skate park	14-15
Safety	16

written by John Lockyer

Skateboarding is fun. It is like roller-skating, surfing and skiing all mixed into one sport. Some skateboarders do tricks.

skateboarding

They sit, kneel, turn and spin on their skateboards. They jump over things and move back and forward.

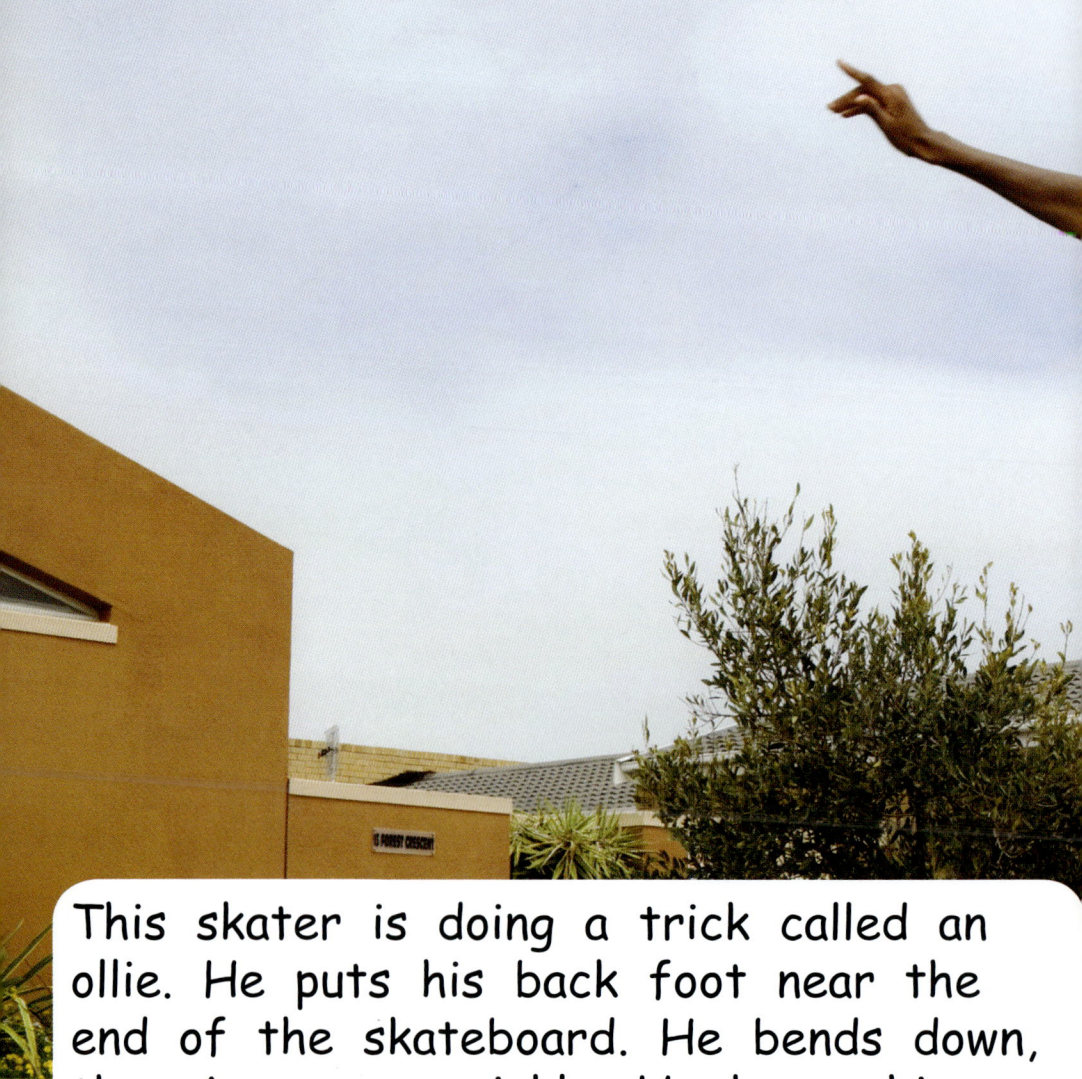

This skater is doing a trick called an ollie. He puts his back foot near the end of the skateboard. He bends down, then jumps up quickly. He keeps his body over the middle of the skateboard, so that it sticks to his feet. When he lands, he bends his knees again.

ollie

A kick flip starts with an ollie. This skater has kicked the skateboard with his foot to make it flip in the air.

He must land with the wheels down so he can ride away safely. Good skateboarders can flip their boards two or three times in the air before they land.

kick flip

This skater is doing a rail slide. No wheels are touching the rail. The bottom of the board is just sliding along the rail.

rail slide

Some skaters put wax on the rails to make the skateboard slide faster.

Some skaters do handstands on a moving skateboard. This skater keeps his head in front of his hands just like a handstand on the ground.

His feet are over his head to give him balance. He doesn't want to crash, so he must look where he is going.

handstand

At a skate park, the skaters have fun together on a ramp or a half-pipe.

half pipe

They ride up and down, going faster and faster. They go so fast that they jump in the air. They kneel, turn, flip, and spin with the other skaters.

This skater is getting up speed. She is using her arms to keep her balance.

skate park

If the skaters fall off, they slide safely across the ground on their knee pads.

Skateboarding is exciting, but it can be dangerous. All good skateboarders wear safety gear. They wear knee pads, elbow pads, gloves, wrist pads, a helmet — and a big smile!